GREAT MOMENTS IN OLYMPIC HISTORY

Olympic Basketball

Adam B. Hofstetter

rosen publishing's
rosen central

New York

For Dad

Published in 2007 by The Rosen Publishing Group, Inc.
29 East 21st Street, New York, NY 10010

First Edition

Library of Congress Cataloging-in-Publication Data

Hofstetter, Adam B.
  Olympic Basketball / Adam B. Hofstetter.
      p. cm. — (Great moments in olympic history)
  Includes bibliographical references.
  ISBN-13: 978-1-4042-0967-1
  ISBN-10: 1-4042-0967-0 (library binding)
  1. Basketball—History—Juvenile literature. 2. Olympics—History—Juvenile literature.
I. Title.
  GV883.H597 2007
  796.323'63-dc22

                                        2006028880

Manufactured in the United States of America

On the cover: American LeBron James drives past Puerto Rico's Sharif Fajardo during a basketball game in the preliminary round of the 2004 Summer Olympics in Athens, Greece. Thanks to advancements in the game's popularity worldwide, the American Olympic men's basketball team is no longer the dominating force it once was.

CONTENTS

CHAPTER 1

The History

The first recorded Olympics, held by the ancient Greeks in 776 B.C., were rather primitive compared to the elaborate ceremonies we are now used to seeing every 2 years. Those first Olympics consisted of only a footrace, but over time more and more events were added. One event they never included, however, was basketball—the game wasn't invented until centuries later. The game of basketball that is played professionally around the world today has changed a lot since it was first invented in 1891.

Basketball first appeared in the Olympics as a demonstration sport in 1904 and was included as an official Olympic event 32 years later. Today, basketball is one of the most popular events at the Summer Olympics. It certainly has come a long way since its early days at the end of the nineteenth century.

One Man's Invention

Unlike many other sports, basketball is not a variation of another sport that already existed. It was invented by Dr. James Naismith. While teaching physical education at the School for Christian Workers in Springfield, Massachusetts—now known as Springfield College—Naismith was instructed by department head Dr. Luther Gulick to come up with "an indoor game that would be interesting, easy to learn, and easy to play in the winter by artificial light." Naismith used peach baskets instead of the nets used today and played the game with a soccer ball on a court that was only about half the size of modern National Basketball Association (NBA) courts. Because the baskets had bottoms, unlike the bottomless nets used today, the ball had to be poked out of the basket with a long stick each time someone scored.

The game proved to be extremely popular and soon spread among YMCAs and colleges. Women's basketball was not far behind. A Smith College teacher named Senda Berenson modified Dr. Naismith's rules to suit women less than a year after Dr. Naismith had first written

Dr. James Naismith was a well-respected college physical education teacher, but he is best known as the man who invented basketball.

5

them down. By the time the first modern Olympics were held in 1896, teams from women's colleges all over the country were playing against other colleges. In 1901, several colleges started men's teams. Before long, hundreds of professional teams were playing basketball throughout the United States.

An Olympic Sport

In 1904, the Olympics were held in St. Louis, Missouri. The games, which were unorganized and spread out over several months, included demonstrations of many sports that were not official Olympic events. One of those was basketball. Six teams, all from the United States, played in what was billed as the "Olympic World's Basket Ball Championship" during the St. Louis games. Two teams from YMCAs dominated the competition. The Buffalo German YMCA of Buffalo, New York, placed first. Some say that makes them the first Olympic basketball champions.

Because the 1904 World's Fair was being held in St. Louis along with the Olympics, basketball was just one of dozens of demonstrations and didn't attract as much attention as it might have at a more organized Olympics. In 1932, eight countries formed the International Basketball Federation (FIBA), an organization that still oversees all international basketball competitions today. The United States joined the group in 1934. Having an international governing body made people take the sport more seriously. In 1936, basketball finally became an official Olympic sport.

Basketball's founding father, Dr. Naismith, was honored by throwing up the opening tip-off at the sport's official Olympic debut. By that point, the sport had become more complicated since he had created the original thirteen rules. Perhaps inspired by Naismith's presence, or simply because the United States had several more years of experience than the rest of the world, the American team won the first Olympic gold medal for basketball.

Dramatic Moments

The American basketball team won the gold medal at every Olympics for the next 32 years. Their streak of seven Olympic championships included an amazing fifty-four consecutive victories in Olympic play. To this day, the U.S. team has remained so dominant that there have been only four Olympic titles won by other countries.

The U.S. team headed to the 1960 Summer Games in Rome, Italy, with what many people at the time believed—and many today still believe—was the best Olympic basketball team of all time. The team—which included several future NBA stars, such as Oscar Robertson and Jerry West—lived up to expectations. The team won every game with an average margin of victory of more than forty-two points. With television broadcasting the Olympics for the first time that year, millions of people witnessed the team's amazing success.

In 1972, the American team faced its toughest challenge yet. They went undefeated through the earlier games but faced a talented Soviet team in the gold-medal game. The game was a battle from start to finish. With only 3 seconds left, the United States led 50-49. The Soviet team had one last chance to retake the lead. Twice they missed their final shot, but each time the officials ruled that the scoreboard clock had to be reset and gave the Soviets another chance. On their third try, the Soviet team finally succeeded, winning the game as time ran out. When the U.S. team lost their appeal of the game's result, the whole team voted to refuse the silver medal in protest. The Americans' amazing winning streak was finally broken.

The Americans came back to win the gold medal at the 1976 games in Montreal, Canada (the Soviets took bronze). But the big story in Olympic basketball that year was women's basketball,

American and Soviet basketball players jump for the ball during their controversial gold-medal game at the 1972 Olympics in Munich. The Americans lost for the first time in Olympic history.

8

which finally made its Olympic debut. Increasing the growing rivalry between the two nations, the Soviet women faced the Americans in the gold-medal game. The Soviets won the gold.

A U.S. boycott of the 1980 Olympics in Moscow led the Soviet Union and several other Communist countries from Europe to sit out the 1984 Summer Games held in Los Angeles, California. With their chief competition staying at home, the United States became the first country to win gold in both men's and women's basketball during the same Olympic Games.

The Rest Is History

We know little about the first Olympics held in ancient Greece. We do know it had only one event—a footrace. Most historians believe the footrace was part of a religious festival to honor Zeus. There was a major temple to Zeus in Olympia, the place where the Olympics were always held, and the Greeks often honored their gods with athletic events.

Athletes and spectators came from all over Greece. For the first thirteen Olympics, the footrace was the sole event. Over time, the Greeks added longer footraces, then other events. The pentathlon and wrestling were the first new sports to be added. The pentathlon included five events: the discus throw, javelin throw, long jump, running, and wrestling. Soon the Olympics included boxing, chariot racing, and riding. There was also the *pankration*, which combined boxing, wrestling, and kicking. After about 300 years, the Olympics included so many events that they lasted for 5 days!

The Olympics continued to be held through the weakening of the Greek empire and the rise of the Roman Empire. Finally, the Roman emperor Theodosius I abolished the games in A.D. 393.

Olympic basketball changed dramatically in 1992, when FIBA changed the rules to allow professional basketball players to compete in the Olympics for the first time. The United States assembled a team of superstars from the NBA that immediately became known as the "Dream Team." The team was so imposing that other countries resigned themselves to playing for the silver medal.

The American women's team was still composed of amateurs because there was no professional league for women. However, the U.S. women's team got the country's attention with their skill and athleticism when they won the gold medal at the 1996 games in Atlanta, Georgia. Soon many members of that gold-medal team were playing professionally in the newly created Women's National Basketball Association (WNBA). The 2000 Olympics featured not one but two Dream Teams from the United States.

The U.S. Dream Teams dominated competition so thoroughly that many observers were left wondering if other countries would ever have another chance at Olympic gold. Their answer came in 2004, when the U.S. men's team was clearly weaker than those of previous years. Argentina took advantage by winning its first ever Olympic medal in basketball.

It has now been more than 100 years since basketball was first

American superstar Lisa Leslie battles an Australian player for the ball during a game at the 1996 Olympics. Leslie led the American women to the gold medal and helped popularize women's basketball.

10

demonstrated at the 1904 Olympics. During that time, the sport has grown from a form of winter exercise to the worldwide sensation it is today. Along the way, it has given Olympic spectators many exciting and dramatic moments. Some have changed or defined the sport, and some have merely been so entertaining that they are still discussed today by basketball fans around the world.

Being Selective

For the 1936 Olympics, the U.S. team was chosen by a group called the American Olympic Basketball Games Committee. The committee invited several top amateur teams in the country for a tournament, then selected players from those teams.

Before the 1956 Olympics, the committee and trials were reorganized. A team of all-stars from the military was invited to the trials. In 1972, sixty-six individual athletes were invited to the Olympic trials, instead of teams.

Four years later, women's basketball was added as an Olympic sport, but the selection process for the women's team was different from that of the men's team. Five regional tryouts were held. Top players were invited to the Olympic Trials, then the final team was selected.

For the 1980 Olympics, the process changed again. A new organization—the Amateur Basketball Association of the United States of America (ABAUSA)—had been established to oversee all national teams for men's and women's basketball. The new organization was officially recognized by FIBA as the United States' national governing body for basketball. Today, the organization is known as USA Basketball.

Another big change came in 1992. Professional players were now allowed in the Olympics, so USA Basketball didn't hold trials for the men's Olympic team. Instead, they used players' performances in the NBA to select the team. With no professional women's league to select from, the women's team still held trials. They did the same for the 1996 team. After the WNBA was formed, the committee adopted the men's format of selecting players based on previous performance instead of trials. This system is still used for both teams today.

CHAPTER 2

Getting Warmed Up

Still a young sport, basketball's popularity took a huge leap forward in 1904 when it was demonstrated by several American teams at the Olympics in St. Louis, Missouri. Six teams competed in what was billed as the "Olympic World's Basket Ball Championship." This was an odd name for the competition because there were only a handful of teams and none of them were from outside the United States.

The competition was split into four events. Each event was a minitournament for a different age group. The main event was called the amateur championships. Two YMCA teams—one from Chicago, Illinois, and one from Buffalo, New York—dominated the competition. The better of the two was the Buffalo German YMCA, which won its first two games by scores of 97-8 and 77-6!

The next level of competition included three college basketball teams, with Hiram College from Ohio winning both its games to claim the championship. Wheaton College, a Christian college from Illinois, came in second. Latter Day Saints University from Utah went winless and ended up in last place.

The difficulty and expense of travel was just one of the many factors that kept the 1904 Olympics from being more successful. This photo shows an automobile parade that was part of the festivities.

13

In both the high school and elementary school competitions, teams from New York and Chicago placed first and second. A team from host city St. Louis placed third out of four high school teams, with a San Francisco team finishing in last place. The elementary school event had only three teams, with third place going to a team from San Francisco.

Since the 1904 World's Fair was held in St. Louis at the same time as the Olympics, basketball was just one of dozens of

Olympic-Sized Mistake

The 1904 Olympics were not a success. They were poorly organized and spread out over several months. The decision to hold the games along with the 1904 World's Fair in St. Louis was a disaster. The World's Fair was an important event back then, so the Olympics got lost in the excitement and Olympic events were not well attended.

The events didn't go smoothly either. The biggest disaster was the marathon, which was run in hot weather over dusty roads. The first man to the finish line was Frederick Lorz, who was hailed as the winner. What the crowd didn't know was that Lorz had dropped out of the race after 9 miles (14 km) and was driven in a car for the next 11 miles (18 km). When the car broke down, Lorz ran the rest of the way. He was discovered after receiving his medal and temporarily banned. Eventual winner Thomas Hicks collapsed near the end of the race. To revive him, his trainers gave him powerful drugs, along with brandy. Hicks almost died from the mixture, but was saved by doctors who treated him at the finish line.

On the way to the Olympics, Cuban postman Felix Carvajal gambled away the money meant to buy shoes and had to race in his street shoes. He stopped often during the race to chat with spectators, stole some peaches from an official, left the race to steal apples from a nearby orchard, and had to take a rest after getting stomach cramps from the fruit. Amazingly, so many runners got disqualified that Carvajal still came in fourth!

Holding the 1904 Olympics in St. Louis along with the World's Fair turned out to be a big mistake. Shown here is the Exhibition ground at the World's Fair.

demonstrations and didn't attract much attention. The sport finally became an official Olympic event in 1936.

The 1936 Berlin Games

Prior to the 1936 games in Berlin, Germany, the United States held trials for the Olympic team in New York's Madison Square Garden. Instead of allowing individual players to attend the trials, invitations were sent to just a handful of the country's top amateur teams. Five college teams—which had all won local championships—were invited, along with the winners of the YMCA national championship and the top two teams from the Amateur Athletic Union (AAU) national championships. A man named Ralph Bishop was the only college player among the fourteen players selected for the Olympic team. Players from the two AAU teams made up the rest of the team, with six players from the AAU champion McPherson Globe Refiners of Kansas and seven from AAU runner-up Universal Pictures of California.

The talented United States team was excited for their first chance at Olympic gold. By 1936, basketball had been played in America for 45 years, but it had only recently achieved wide international popularity. Teams from other countries were still struggling to catch up to the more experienced Americans. The U.S. team was the early favorite at the 1936 games.

When the players arrived in Berlin, they were informed of several rule changes that had been made 2 years earlier at a FIBA meeting that U.S. representatives had not attended. Each team was now limited to only seven players a game. To obey, U.S. head coach Jim Needles had to split his team into two seven-man groups, one with the seven players from Universal and one with the six players from McPherson plus Ralph Bishop. The two groups alternated from game to game.

The new rules seemed specifically designed to prevent the U.S. team from success. One obvious example was a rule banning players taller than 6 feet 2 inches (1.9 m). Several players on the U.S. team were over the height limit, including their two tallest players, Joe Fortenberry and Willard Schmidt, who were both 6 feet 8 inches (2 m) tall. That rule was so unreasonable that it was withdrawn as soon as the United States complained. In spite of being treated unfairly, the Americans began a fifty-four-game Olympic winning streak that would last 32 years.

Gold for the United States

Spain was supposed to be the Americans' first opponent. However, the Spanish team did not attend the Olympics because Spain was engaged in a civil war. The United States won by forfeit. The American team then faced the European champions, Estonia, without a first-round game as a warm-up. Going into the game cold didn't seem to matter for the seven players from Universal. They beat Estonia by a score of 52-28. The McPherson players had similar success, beating the Philippine team 56-23. In the next game, Mexico's team held the Americans to just 25 points. However, Mexico scored only 10 points of their own, and the U.S. team advanced to the finals against Canada.

At the 1936 Olympic Games—just like at every previous Olympics—all events were held outdoors. That meant events could

The bronze medal–winning Mexican team faces off against the Philippines during the 1936 Olympics. It was the first year that basketball was an official Olympic sport.

be dramatically affected by the weather. A perfect example of this was the 1936 basketball final. The outdoor court was made of sand and clay, and it rained before the gold-medal game. Playing on the mushy, muddy surface as the rain continued, both teams had trouble scoring. Center Joe Fortenberry of the McPherson players led all scorers with 8 points as the Americans secured the very first Olympic gold medal in basketball with a 19-8 win.

Basketball's inventor, Dr. James Naismith, had the honor of presenting basketball's first Olympic medals. It was a great moment for the sport of basketball. Just 45 years after Naismith had nailed up those first peach baskets, basketball had cemented its place as an Olympic event and as one of the most popular sports around the world. Naismith died 3 years later, having seen his invention grow from a fun new gym exercise for college students into an international sensation.

As excited as the American team was to bring home the gold, the victory was somewhat bittersweet. Because of the seven-player limit, only those seven players who had played in the final game were given medals. Clearly FIBA was doing everything it could to prevent the country that invented the sport from dominating international play. But that's exactly what happened in the first official Olympic basketball competition in spite of the many obstacles. America's supremacy in Olympic basketball would continue for the next few decades.

CHAPTER 3

Best Ever

When asked to name the best Olympic basketball team ever, most people immediately think of the 1992 Dream Team that featured NBA superstars such as Michael Jordan and Larry Bird. But before many members of the 1992 squad were even born, the United States assembled a team so talented that experts still regard it as the greatest team of all time.

In contrast to the 1992 team of NBA greats, the 1960 U.S. men's basketball team was assembled entirely of amateur players. The twelve-man roster included such future NBA legends as Oscar Robertson, Jerry West, and Jerry Lucas, plus standouts like Walt Bellamy and Terry Dischinger. Ten members of the team went on to play in the NBA. Four players were later named NBA Rookie of the Year. Three of those were elected to the Basketball Hall of Fame, as was another member of the 1960 team.

As impressive as the players' talent was the team's depth and balance. Despite the talent of the starters, head coach Pete Newell used his bench liberally and with great success. Five U.S. players averaged more than 10 points per game in the Olympics, and everyone on the roster contributed. Imagine a team so talented that not even the great Oscar Robertson—one of the greatest basketball players of all time—became a dominant star in the tournament.

The Amazing Jerry West

Jerry West was small for a basketball player and not particularly strong. That didn't stop him from becoming one of the greatest guards ever to play basketball at any level. West was too small to play in junior high school. At East Bank High School in West Virginia, he sat on the bench until he suddenly grew 6 inches (15 cm) during the summer before his senior year. With his can't-miss jump shot and new height, West became the team's star player almost overnight. He quickly broke state scoring records and carried East Bank to the state title in 1956. At West Virginia University, he was twice named All-American—an honor given to the best college players—and brought the team

Before helping the U.S. men's basketball team win the Olympic gold medal in 1960, Jerry West was a star player at West Virginia University.

21

to the 1959 NCAA championship, where he scored more points than any other player in the tournament.

West was drafted by the Minneapolis Lakers in the first round of the 1960 NBA Draft just before the team moved to Los Angeles. The Lakers played in the NBA Finals 9 out of the 14 years West was on the team and finally won the championship in 1972.

Nicknamed "Mr. Clutch," West was an All-Star every year of his career, an honor awarded to professional basketball players by basketball fans. He was also named Most Valuable Player (MVP) of the 1969 Finals, the only player from a losing team ever to earn such an honor. By the time he retired, he was the third-leading scorer of all time. West was elected to the Basketball Hall of Fame in 1979. To this day, his image is featured in the NBA logo.

The Big O

Fellow Olympic teammate Oscar Robertson first caught the attention of basketball scouts when he played for Crispus Attucks High School in Indianapolis, Indiana. Thanks in large part to him, the team won forty-five straight games and became the first African American school to win the Indiana state

The University of Cincinnati's Oscar Robertson was the National College Player of the Year three times before joining the 1960 U.S. Olympic team.

championship and the national championship. At the University of Cincinnati, Robertson was the first player to lead the NCAA in scoring three times and the first to be named National College Player of the Year three times. The U.S. Basketball Writers Association later renamed the award after him.

After "The Big O" graduated in 1960 and cocaptained the 1960 Olympic team, the Cincinnati Royals made him the first overall pick in the 1960 NBA Draft. His dominance in every aspect of the game led him to Rookie of the Year honors in 1961 and the league MVP award in 1964. In 1971, he helped lead the Milwaukee Bucks to the only NBA championship in their history. By the time he retired, he was the all-time leader in career assists and free throws, and was second in scoring. He also owned several rebounding records. He is generally considered the best all-around player in NBA history and was elected to the Basketball Hall of Fame shortly after retiring.

Jerry Lucas

West and Robertson were accompanied by Jerry Lucas, a superstar in his own right who was an accurate shooter and even better at rebounding and passing. Lucas was just 20 years old when he joined the Olympic team, but had already established himself as one of the best college players in the country. After guiding his high school team to seventy-six consecutive wins and two state titles, he was named All-American three times at Ohio State University. Lucas led the Ohio State Buckeyes to the national title in 1960 just a few months before heading to Rome for the Olympic Games. He was named National College Player of the Year in 1961 and 1962 and was considered the best college player of all time when he graduated. His success continued in the NBA, where he was named Rookie of the Year in 1964, played on seven All-Star teams, and was eventually named to the Basketball Hall of Fame.

A Wealth of Talent

Robertson, West, and Lucas may have been the most famous of the twelve men on the 1960 Olympic squad, but the team's talent didn't end there. Starting center Walt Bellamy went on to an impressive NBA career that included Rookie of the Year honors and election to the Basketball Hall of Fame. Forward Terry Dischinger also won the NBA's Rookie of the Year award and was a three-time All-Star. Bob Boozer was an All-American forward for Kansas State University in 1958 and 1959 and went on to a successful NBA career.

Then there was Jay Arnette, who was an outstanding baseball player at the University of Texas and also led the UT basketball team to the conference championship in 1960 before joining the Olympic team. Point guard Adrian Smith, the fifth-leading scorer on the 1960 Olympic team, won an NCAA championship with the University of Kentucky and scored 24 points in just 26 minutes in the 1966 NBA All-Star Game. Burdette Haldorson had already won a gold medal with the American team at the 1956 games. Backup center Darral Imhoff was twice named All-American for the University of California, Berkeley, where he made the shot that won the NCAA championship. He played twelve seasons in the NBA.

The Superstars of 1960

The United States was the clear favorite heading into the Olympics. The team lived up to expectations, bulldozing host Italy by a score of 88-54 in the opening game. Smith and Robertson each scored 16 points. The next victim was Japan, who fell by a score of 125-66, including 28 points from Lucas. Then came a 107-63 victory over Hungary thanks to 22 points from Robertson and 21 from Lucas. The semifinals against Yugoslavia were more of the same,

The height of the American players was just one of their many weapons in 1960. Here they are towering over the Brazilians in the gold-medal game.

25

New Technology

The 1960 Olympic Games were remarkable in many ways. Brand-new facilities were custom-built for the occasion. For the first time, broadcast television offered complete coverage of the games. Eurovision broadcast many events live throughout Europe, and CBS covered them for the United States. However, it was not yet possible to broadcast the games live back to the United States, so CBS taped their broadcasts and flew the tapes by plane to New York every day.

and this time it was Dischinger leading the attack with 16 points in a decisive 104-42 win. They outscored Uruguay 108-50 next, and Smith led all scorers with 15 points.

The next game was their first real test. They matched up against a powerful Soviet team that included 7-foot-3-inch (2.2-m) center Jan Kruminsh. The game was close in the first half, but the Americans pulled away in the second half. Thanks in part to West's 19 points, they beat the Soviets by "only" 24 points. Playing Italy again, the U.S. team's balance and depth truly shone through. Six U.S. players scored in the double digits as they beat Italy 112-81. They faced Brazil in the gold-medal game. Another 25 points from Lucas led to a 90-63 victory, a perfect 8-0 record in Rome, and yet another gold medal. The team averaged more than 100 points per game in the tournament and, on average, scored over 42 points more than their opponents!

Where Are They Now?

Most members of the 1960 team joined the NBA shortly after the Olympics, but followed different paths once their playing careers were over.

Some, like Jerry West, stayed in basketball as executives. After retiring from the NBA, West was hired by the Lakers as a coach and proved to be just as talented off the court as he was on it. In 1982, he became an executive with the team, and the Lakers won seven championships over the next 20 years. West then took a job as president of basketball operations for the Memphis Grizzlies, a position he still holds today.

Oscar Robertson has spent his post-NBA career as an activist and businessman. He cofounded the National Basketball Retired Players Association and served as president for several years. In addition to brief periods in broadcasting and coaching basketball, Robertson's business endeavors include banking, construction, the food industry, and a media company that published a basketball instruction book he wrote. He also works with the National Kidney Foundation, and in 1997 donated one of his kidneys to his daughter Tia. In 2003, he wrote a best-selling autobiography and received the University of Cincinnati's highest honor for alumni.

Jerry Lucas turned his love of memory tricks, word games, and magic into a new career as an entertainer. He hosted a television special called *The Jerry Lucas Super Kids Day Magic Jamboree*. He once appeared on national TV, where he displayed his memory skills by memorizing 500 pages of a phone book. In 1974, he coauthored *The Memory Book*—an instructional book on improving memory that sold more than 2 million copies. Since then, he has written more than thirty memory books. He also founded Lucas Learning, Inc., an educational publishing company focusing on teaching children how to build memory skills.

CHAPTER 4

Russian Rivalry

The United States and the Soviet Union had been involved in a cold war since the 1960s, and tension between the two powerful nations emerged in many areas. The enemies had competing weapons programs, competing space programs, and—yes—competing basketball programs. The situation worsened between the national basketball teams in 1972, when a series of controversial calls by referees took the Olympic gold medal out of the hands of one team and gave it to the other.

The American team arrived at the 1972 Summer Olympics in Munich, Germany, as the youngest group to ever represent the United States at the Olympics. The United States had won every gold medal since basketball had become an Olympic sport. In fact, they had won every Olympic game they had ever played. With such an impressive streak and yet another talented roster, they were the favorites once again to win in Munich. However, the Soviet team was talented, bigger, and more experienced.

The Americans breezed through their first eight games in Munich, winning seven of them with double-digit victories. The Soviets made quick work of their first eight opponents as well, and nobody was surprised when they advanced to the gold-medal game. The fight for the gold medal would be the toughest the U.S. team had ever faced.

Trouble in Munich

The Soviets' slow style of play threw the fast-running Americans off their game. At halftime, the Soviet Union led by 5 points. In the second half, their lead grew to 10 points with only a few minutes left to play. Suddenly the Americans found new life through guard Kevin Joyce, who led a late attack that shrunk the difference in scores to a single point. With just a few seconds left to play, American guard Doug Collins caught a pass thrown by the Soviet team and was fouled on his way to the basket. He hit

When the game clock ran down, the Americans thought they had won the gold medal. Here they celebrate their victory moments before being told that the Soviets would have another chance to shoot the winning basket.

29

both free throws, giving the United States its first lead of the game, 50-49, with just 3 seconds remaining.

A Long Shot

The Soviets had one last chance to score, but it would literally be a long shot. They would have to race down the entire court and get off a shot in just 3 seconds. The referees stopped the clock with 1 second left when the Soviets called a time-out. One second wouldn't be enough time to score; the game appeared to be over. The Soviets argued that they had called for the time-out before Collins' two free throws, so there should still be 3 seconds left. The referees agreed, and the clock was reset to 3 seconds.

The Americans were furious, but had little choice but to play out the final 3 seconds one more time. Play had barely started again before the clock ran out. The final buzzer sounded, and the U.S. team once again started celebrating its victory. This lasted only moments, because officials ordered the teams back on the floor. The clock had not been properly reset before the play started. The Soviets would get a third chance to score the winning basket.

Soviet forward Alexander Belov jumped up to catch a full-court pass and made the basket as time ran out. The United States had lost their first Olympic basketball game ever. The Americans, disgusted by what they thought was favoritism toward the Soviets, filed a formal protest with FIBA. Later that

While the Soviet team accepted their gold medals, the platform for the second-place Americans remained empty as U.S. players protested the results by skipping the ceremony.

day, a five-member panel of FIBA judges upheld the results of the game. Olympic basketball had a new champion.

The Americans, believing that they had been cheated out of the gold medal, refused to attend the medal ceremony or to accept their silver medals. Those silver medals still sit, unclaimed, in a vault in Lausanne, Switzerland. They are a dusty symbol of a bitter rivalry between two world powers and two talented basketball teams.

The 1976 Montreal Games

The rivalry only intensified at the next Olympics. Women's basketball finally made its Olympic debut at the 1976 games in Montreal, Canada. The Soviet women came to Montreal having not lost a game at a major international competition in 18 years. The U.S. team had a perfect 5-0 record in the Olympic qualifying rounds and was also eyeing the gold medal.

Tough teams stood in their way. First came Japan, which handed the Americans an 84-71 defeat. The U.S. women recovered to beat Bulgaria and Canada. However, their next opponent was the Soviet Union, which had won all of its games. Towering Soviet center Jullana Semenova averaged almost 20 points per game.

The much-anticipated matchup between the Americans and Soviets turned out to be no contest. The Soviet women stormed to a 112-77 victory and went on to win all five of their games and the first ever gold medal in women's basketball. The Americans, meanwhile, beat Czechoslovakia 83-67 to secure the silver.

The U.S. women hadn't beaten their chief rivals and wouldn't get another chance in 1980 due to a U.S. boycott of the Olympics, held in Moscow. The Soviet Union then refused to attend the 1984 Summer Olympics in Los Angeles, California.

Basketball Comes Home

The year 1984 marked the first time Olympic basketball was played in the country where the game was invented. The Soviets and other Communist nations boycotted the games, so the American teams had little competition. Led by legendary Indiana University coach Bobby Knight and future NBA superstars

Michael Jordan and Patrick Ewing, the American men blew past China, Canada, Uruguay, France, Spain, and West Germany. Facing Canada again, the United States won by 19 points and advanced to the gold-medal game against Spain. The Americans won the gold medal 96-65.

Cheryl Miller, shown here playing for the University of Southern California against the Stanford Cardinals, helped lead the U.S. women's team to the Olympic gold medal in 1984.

Meanwhile, the American women destroyed every team that stood between them and their long-awaited gold medal. Led by the legendary Cheryl Miller, they beat Yugoslavia 83-55. Huge victories over Australia, South Korea, China, and Canada followed. In the gold-medal game, they defeated South Korea by 30 points.

The U.S. women had their first Olympic gold medal and the United States became the first country to win gold medals in both men's and women's basketball. In spite of both teams' lack of real competition, it was a major achievement for USA Basketball. It also gave three players—Michael Jordan, Patrick Ewing, and Chris Mullin—valuable Olympic experience that would come in handy 8 years later.

CHAPTER 5

Dream Sequence

In what might be the biggest rule change to date, FIBA began allowing professional players to compete in the Olympics in 1989. The timing of the decision meant that 1992 would be the first Olympics to feature professional basketball players. That one decision changed the entire face of Olympic basketball.

At the time, several countries had professional basketball leagues, but the United States' pro league was widely acknowledged to be the best. Basketball fans nationwide were excited about an Olympic squad that would essentially be an NBA all-star team, and they weren't disappointed when the team roster was announced. Many of the players—such as Earvin "Magic" Johnson, Michael Jordan, Patrick Ewing, Larry Bird, and Charles Barkley—were not merely the best current players. They were among the greatest players of all time.

The Dream Team

Right from the start, this Dream Team was favored to win the gold medal at the 1992 games in Barcelona, Spain. They plowed through the qualifying round unbeaten, and people stopped talking about whether the team was beatable and talked instead about whether any other team would even come close. The answer to that question appeared to be no as the Dream Team destroyed Angola in the first round by a score of 116-48. Croatia, the next opponent, featured Croatian-born NBA star Tony Kukoc. That game was slightly tougher, but the U.S. team managed to win by 33 points. The next victim was Germany, followed by Brazil and Spain.

The quarterfinals were more of the same as Puerto Rico fell 115-77. Up next was Lithuania in the semifinals. The Lithuanian team boasted four of the top six scorers from the 1988 gold medal–winning Soviet team,

Michael Jordan's acrobatics, as seen in this game against Spain, helped the American "Dream Team" dominate the competition in 1992.

The U.S. men's team accepts their gold medals, the first ever won by professional basketball players.

but even they proved no match for the American stars. An incredible nine U.S. players scored in double figures as they beat the Lithuanians 127-76.

The gold-medal game was against Croatia again. Again, the Americans beat Kukoc and his team by more than 30 points—32 to be exact. Amazingly, that was the closest any team had come to beating the Americans. With an average margin of victory of almost 44 points and an 8-0 record at the games, the U.S. team won perhaps the most conclusive gold medal in Olympic history.

"You will see a team of professionals in the Olympics again," U.S. coach Chuck Daly said later. "But I don't think you'll see another team quite like this. This was a majestic team."

The Women Go for Gold

Before long, the men's U.S. basketball team wasn't the only Dream Team. People knew that the U.S. women's basketball team was going to be tough when they came out of training with a record of fifty-two wins and no losses. The team's dominance in the run-up to the 1996 Summer Games caught the country's attention. With the games held on American soil in Atlanta, Georgia, record numbers of fans bought tickets for the team's Olympic contests. Their first game was sold out. In that game, Cuba jumped out to an early 7-point lead. The Americans soon struck back. Every player on the U.S. team scored as they handed Cuba a decisive 101-84 defeat. They beat the Ukraine 98-65, then defeated Zaire by a U.S. Olympic record margin of 60 points—107-47.

About 34,000 fans were on hand for the next game, and the American team sent the record crowd home happy by beating the Australian team by 17 points. Next came a big 105-64 win over South Korea. In the quarterfinals, the Americans' height advantage over the smaller Japanese players helped them to a 108-93 victory.

The U.S. women faced Australia again in the semifinals and quickly learned that the Australians had made some adjustments in their playing since the teams' first game. After the first 6 minutes, Australia led 18-10. The Americans then went on a 27-4 run, putting the game out of reach for the Australians before it ended in a 93-71 American victory.

The American women had won all seven of their games at that point, but so had the Brazilians—the same team that had knocked the Americans out of the 1994 World Championships. The gold-medal game between the two teams drew another huge crowd to the Georgia Dome. Those fans saw a U.S. team that practically couldn't miss, hitting almost 72 percent of their shots in the first half on the way to an 11-point lead. They widened their lead by starting the second half with 8 points, and walked away with a 111-87 victory and the gold medal. Again, all twelve members of the team scored.

The team's success got the American public excited about women's basketball and awakened them to the depth of talent in the women's game. The women's team drew more than 200,000 fans to just eight games, and the average of 25,320 fans per game was more than most NBA teams were drawing at regular season games. The success of the Olympic team and the public's interest led the NBA to back a new professional league that would closely parallel the men's league. On June 21, 1997, just months after the U.S. women wowed the Georgia Dome crowds, the Los Angeles Sparks hosted the New York Liberty in the WNBA's first game.

Lisa Leslie and Venus Lacey celebrate their victory over Brazil in the gold-medal game at the 1996 Olympics.

Cooper and the Comets

After the U.S. women's basketball team won gold at the 1996 games, basketball fans were hungry for more. The WNBA was created the following year, and their first season was a huge success. Though the WNBA's high-profile players weren't yet as famous as NBA superstars such as Michael Jordan and Patrick Ewing, the women were about to step into the spotlight once again.

On August 30, 1997, the Houston Comets went up against the New York Liberty in the WNBA's first ever championship game in front of 16,285 excited fans. A few seconds before the final buzzer sounded, the Houston Comets began celebrating their 65-51 defeat of the New York Liberty and their status as the first WNBA Champions.

The Comets' superstar guard, Cynthia Cooper, who played on both the 1988 and 1992 Olympic teams, was the game's high scorer with 25 points, four rebounds, and four assists. Cooper had been the WNBA's leading scorer, had been named MVP of the regular season, and snagged a second MVP award during the championship game.

"I never would have imagined when the season began that I would be in this position," Cooper said after the game. "It feels great to accomplish this in a team atmosphere after so many sacrifices this summer."

39

The Dream Team Gets a Wake-up Call

America's Dream Teams continued their success in later Olympic Games. The women repeated as Olympic champions in 2000 and 2004. The men's team won gold in 1996 and again in 2000, but the victories for the men were growing less decisive. Some critics blamed selfish players, saying they played as twelve individuals rather than as a team. Others complained of flaws in the American game in general. Some critics said American players chose style over substance, unlike players who learned the game in other countries where fundamentals are given more importance.

All three factors likely played a part in the Dream Team's eventual wake-up call in 2004. The world's teams had improved considerably since the American men's team had stomped the competition in 1992. More foreign players were succeeding in the NBA than ever before. By the time the 2004 games began in Athens, Greece, the U.S. team was just one of several strong teams competing for the gold medal.

The United States Struggles to Stay in the Game

The Americans' first opponent was Puerto Rico, a team they had handled easily in various competitions over the previous year. The U.S. team couldn't find their shooting touch, missing more than 65 percent of their shots in a 92-73 loss. It was the United States' first Olympic loss since they began using professional players.

Even with one of their star players injured (Allen Iverson had broken his thumb), the loss to Puerto Rico was embarrassing for the Americans.

In their next game, the U.S. team barely won against host Greece with a score of 77-71. Then came another hard-earned victory, this time a 10-point win over Australia. Up next was Lithuania. This game was close as well. Lithuania was behind by 5 points with just 3 minutes to play, but came back to defeat the Americans 94-90.

The Americans finished out the first round by crushing a weak Angola team 89-53. With a record of three wins and two losses in the first round of play, the U.S. team ended up in fourth place,

The United States lost to Lithuania in an early round but defeated them to win the bronze medal. Here, American Tim Duncan drives to the basket as Lithuanians Darius Songaila and Ramunas Siskauskas try to stop him.

41

meaning they'd have to play the top-ranked team in the quarter-finals. It was the lowest ranking the U.S. team had ever earned, but their medal hopes were still alive. Top-ranked Spain was 5-0, but American Stephon Marbury scored a U.S. Olympic record 31 of his team's 102 points, leading his team to victory. The entire team had regained its shooting touch, and just in time.

For the semifinals, the Americans matched up against an Argentinian team that was almost unchanged since handing the United States a crushing defeat in the 2002 World Championships. The game was tight from start to finish. Marbury scored 18 points and teammate Lamar Odom added 14, but it wasn't enough. Argentina held the Americans to scoring less than just 42 percent of their shots and defeated them 89-81.

Argentina Reigns Supreme

The U.S. team was able to salvage a bronze medal by taking revenge on Lithuania, winning the bronze-medal game by a final score of 104-96. However, the team's top scorer for the entire tournament, Iverson, was outscored by eleven Olympians from other nations. Throughout the tournament, the Americans rebounded well with plenty of assists and blocked shots, but their poor shooting finally did them in. The bronze medal was an enormous disappointment for a country that had not only invented the sport but had dominated it up until that point.

Argentina, meanwhile, still had work to do. Defeating the Americans was certainly exciting, but they wanted gold. They had lost the championship game in overtime at the 2002 World Championships and were not about to let a title slip away from them again. Facing Italy in the gold-medal game, they pulled out a decisive 84-69 victory to win Argentina's first Olympic medal for basketball.

With new basketball powers emerging from all over the globe, the face of basketball is still changing. It certainly is a far cry from the 1904 games, when a handful of Americans from a couple of amateur teams first introduced basketball to the world.

Members of Argentina's men's basketball team celebrate their first Olympic gold medal on August 28, 2004.

43

Timeline

776 B.C.	First recorded ancient Olympics are held. Only event is a footrace.
1891	Dr. James Naismith invents basketball.
1892	Senda Berenson modifies Dr. Naismith's rules to apply to women. Women's colleges begin to form teams.
1901	Colleges begin to form men's teams.
1904	St. Louis, Missouri: Basketball debuts as a demonstration sport at Olympics. Six U.S. teams play in "Olympic World's Basket Ball Championship" during St. Louis games.
1932	International Basketball Federation (FIBA) is formed.
1936	Berlin, Germany: Basketball becomes an official Olympic event. Basketball's inventor, Dr. James Naismith, throws tip-off. The U.S. team wins the gold medal.
1960	Rome, Italy: Widely believed to be the best ever Olympic basketball team, the United States wins the gold medal, with an average margin of victory of more than 42 points.
1972	Munich, Germany: The Soviet Union defeats the United States in the final seconds of a gold-medal game that is still a subject of disagreement.
1976	Montreal, Canada: Women's basketball becomes an official Olympic event. The Soviet team wins the gold medal, and the U.S. team wins the silver medal.
1984	Los Angeles, California: With the Soviet Union boycotting the Olympic Games, the United States becomes the first country to win gold medals in both men's and women's basketball.
1992	Barcelona, Spain: FIBA allows professionals to play in the Olympics for the first time. The U.S. "Dream Team" of NBA players wins the gold medal. The U.S. women's team wins the bronze medal.
1996	Atlanta, Georgia: The U.S. women's team wins the gold medal, leading to the creation of the Women's National Basketball Association (WNBA).
2000	Sydney, Australia: The U.S. men's and women's teams both win gold medals.
2004	Athens, Greece: Argentina defeats the U.S. men's team and wins their first ever gold medal in basketball. The United States wins the bronze medal. The U.S. women's team wins the gold medal.

Glossary

activist A person who works to further a specific belief or cause.

alumni Graduates or former students of a school, college, or university.

amateur An athlete who does not accept money for playing a sport.

appeal A request to have a case heard again before a higher court.

boycott To protest something by refusing to use, buy, or take part in it.

cold war A condition of rivalry, mistrust, and sometimes open hostility between two large power groups, such as the condition that existed between the United States and Soviet Union from the late 1940s to 1991, when the Soviet Union collapsed.

Communist Having a system of government in which all property, the means of production, and the system of distribution of goods are controlled by the state.

consecutive Following one after another without interruption.

debut A first appearance.

demonstration A public display.

draft A system in which professional sports teams choose new players.

forfeit To lose something or have to give it up.

rookie A player in his or her first year of professional sports.

roster A list of names of members of a team.

tip-off The act of putting the ball in play in basketball by a jump ball.

Soviet Relating to the country once known as the Soviet Union. Today, much of what was the Soviet Union is known as Russia.

supremacy Power to dominate or defeat.

For More Information

AAU National Headquarters
P.O. Box 22409
Lake Buena Vista, FL 32830
Phone: 407-934-7200
Web site: http://www.aausports.org

International Basketball Federation (FIBA)
Avenue Louis Casaï, 53
1216 Cointrin
Geneva
Switzerland
Phone: 41-22-545-00-00
Web site: http://www.fiba.com

Naismith Memorial Basketball Hall of Fame
1000 West Columbus Avenue
Springfield, MA 01105
Phone: 413-781-6500
Web site: http://www.hoophall.com

National Basketball Association (NBA)
Olympic Tower
645 Fifth Avenue
New York, NY 10022
Phone: 212-407-8000
Web site: http://www.nba.com

National Collegiate Athletics Association (NCAA)
700 W. Washington Street
P.O. Box 6222
Indianapolis, IN 46206-6222
Phone: 317-917-6222
Web site: http://www.ncaa.org

USA Basketball
5465 Mark Dabling Boulevard
Colorado Springs, CO 80918-3842
Phone: 719-590-4800
Email: FanMail@usabasketball.com
Web site: http://www.usabasketball.com

Women's National Basketball Association (WNBA)
Olympic Tower
645 Fifth Avenue
New York, NY 10022
Phone: 212-688-9622
Web site: http://www.wnba.com

Web Sites

Due to the changing nature of Internet links, the Rosen Publishing Group, Inc., has developed an online list of Web sites related to the subject of this book. This site is updated regularly. Please use this link to access the list: http://www.rosenlinks.com/gmoh/bask

For Further Reading

DK Publishing. *Basketball*. New York: DK Publishing, 2005.

Fischer, David. *The Encyclopedia of the Summer Olympics*. Princeton, NJ: Franklin Watts, 2004.

Giglio, Joe. *Great Teams in Pro Basketball History*. Oxford, Great Britain: Raintree Publishers, 2006.

Lannin, Joanne. *A History of Basketball for Girls and Women: From Bloomers to Big Leagues*. Minneapolis, MN: LernerSports, 2000.

Layden, Joe. *Superstars of U.S.A. Women's Basketball*. New York: Simon & Schuster Children's Publishing, 2000.

Robertson, Oscar. *The Big O: My Life, My Times, My Game*. Emmaus, PA: Rodale Books, 2003.

Stewart, Mark. *Basketball: A History of Hoops*. Princeton, NJ: Franklin Watts, 1999.

Wolff, Alexander. *Big Game, Small World: A Basketball Adventure*. New York: Warner Books, 2002.

Bibliography

Daly, Chuck, and Alex Sachare. *America's Dream Team: The Quest for Olympic Gold*. Atlanta, GA: Turner Publishing, 1992.

Hubbard, Jan, ed. *The Official NBA Basketball Encyclopedia*, 3rd ed. New York: Doubleday, 2000.

Miller, Ernestine. *Making Her Mark: Firsts and Milestones in Women's Sports*. New York: Contemporary Books, 2002.

Pound, Dick. *Inside the Olympics: A Behind-the-Scenes Look at the Politics, the Scandals, and the Glory of the Games*. Mississauga, Canada: John Wiley & Sons Canada, Ltd., 2004.

Roberts, Randy. *But They Can't Beat Us: Oscar Robertson and the Crispus Attucks Tigers*. Champaign, IL: Sagamore Publishing, 1999.

Robertson, Oscar. *The Big O: My Life, My Times, My Game*. New York: Rodale Books, 2003.

Schaffer, Kay, and Sidonie Smith, eds. *The Olympics at the Millennium: Power, Politics, and the Games*. Piscataway, NJ: Rutgers University Press, 2000.

Smith, Lissa, ed. *Nike Is a Goddess: The History of Women in Sports*. New York: Atlantic Monthly Press, 1998.

Spivey, Nigel. *The Ancient Olympics: A History*. New York: Oxford University Press, 2004.

Stauth, Cameron. *Golden Boys: An Unauthorized Look at the U.S. Olympic Basketball Team*. New York: Atria Books, 1992.

Wallechinsky, David. *The Complete Book of the Summer Olympics: Athens 2004 Edition*. Toronto, Canada: SPORTClassic Books, 2004.

West, Jerry, and Bill Libby. *Mr. Clutch: The Jerry West Story*. Englewood Cliffs, NJ: Prentice-Hall, 1969.

Young, David C. *A Brief History of the Olympic Games*. Oxford, Great Britain: Blackwell Publishing, 2004.

the big O.com
http://www.thebigo.com

Doctor Memory
http://www.jerrylucas.com/

HickokSports.com: Sports History–Olympic Basketball
http://www.hickoksports.com/history/olbask.shtml

USA Basketball
http://www.usabasketball.com

WNBA
http://www.wnba.com

Index

About the Author

Adam Hofstetter is a weekly columnist for SportsIllustrated.com. He has written three other sports books for Rosen Publishing. When he's not attending various sports events, Adam can be found in Cedarhurst, New York, where he lives with his wife, Sarah, and their two children, Abby and Sam.

Photo Credits

Cover © Andy Lyons/Getty Images; pp. 5, 13, 15, 18, 21, 22 © Hulton Archive/ Getty Images; p. 8 © Getty Images; p. 9 © Michael Steele/Getty Images; p. 10 © Al Bello/Allsport; p. 25 © Central Press/Getty Images; p. 29 © AFP/Getty Images; p. 31 © Bettmann/Corbis; pp. 33, 36 © Mike Powell/Allsport; p. 35 © Dimitri Messinis/AFP/Getty Images; p. 38 © Doug Pensi/Getty Images; p. 39 © Todd Warshaw/Getty Images; p. 41 © Mladen Antonov/AFP/Getty Images; p. 43 © Jamie Squire/Getty Images.

Designer: Daniel Hosek
Editor: Kerri O'Donnell